Piñata Theory

Piñata Theory

ALAN CHAZARO

Black
Lawrence
Press

Black
Lawrence
Press

www.blacklawrence.com

Executive Editor: Diane Goettel
Chapbook Editor: Kit Frick
Cover Design: Zoe Norvel
Cover Art: PIÑATA Y DULCES by Francisco Palomares.
Book Design: Amy Freels

Published 2020 by Black Lawrence Press.
Printed in the United States.

For

Abigail & Francisco & Monica & Ignacio & Aldo & Sasha & Gary & Lala & Yayo &
Kristian & Sophia & Serge & Lalita & Adrian & Carlos & Sergio & Raymundo & Lois
& Teresa & Briana

Contents

Gather

Psychoanalysis of a Piñata

The fault line between me runs north

      from south, a zag

splitting my skull and bursting
my edges. These ribs are ridges

rubbing dangerous—

      friction
to make worlds
shake with color. There is movement
within—

      these earthquakes
my unfinished

therapy. I make sweetness
out of fractures, make fire

      dance from teeth,
my shape

an ash-bound phoenix. Tonight

I live to be undone—

Body

Body

Body

Body

Body

Body

Body

Body

Body

Body

Body

Body

Body

Body

Body

Body

Body

Body

Body

Body

Body

Body

Body

Translations from the Backseat of a Colectivo in Oaxaca

We jump into the cab and suddenly we're moving somewhere and somehow silence becomes the driver talking mezcal and illegal rooster fights, and he is telling Adrian about a party in Mitla tomorrow night, where *la raza se pone a pistear*, where you drink the hours away until you fall into a stranger's house, and the next morning you wake up to watch the men playing *fút, pero bien crudo*. His instructions: take a shot, then down your beer, then rinse it with mezcal before blowing the smoke from your mouth. Just like that. And if you can still stand and chase the soccer ball rolling across a dirt field faster than locals, you've mastered something. *Así que tienes que entrenar por un año* until you gain the gut-strength required to last around here. And I'm watching the desert, or maybe the desert is watching me, but either way we are speeding past adobe, past fields of maguey, past a valley where this compa tells us the pumas will hunt you if you stray too far off at night. I don't see any pumas, only signs of *Yaguar Xoo* and *Tlacolula*, pointing to nowhere I've been. And Adrian tells us about the time he crossed a desert, somewhere above Arizona, beneath a mirror of his country. How his dad, Niceforo, was detained on one side, his eyes bordered with questions. They exchanged a wad of cash and *don't-be-afraids* that night to get past the hours separating darkness from more darkness. The story doesn't end there but the driver doesn't stop talking about Zapotec ruins, about the teachers who fired up a strike until they were struck down, about petrified waterfalls we should visit. *La cuidad de los muertos* he calls it, where they harvest the best-tasting fruits you won't find anywhere else. He laughs, we'd need more than this lifetime to find what's in these mountains, these majestic bones. I'm in the middle, speechless, listening. I'm learning how to touch my mouth without being swallowed. I am opening. The story doesn't end there.

Reading Autobiographies

The summer I was saved I was sitting
on cobblestone steps in Xalapa
while Massive Attack played inside

my headphones, Sasha beside me
as a family of clouds lazed
above the Catholic church steeple

at the center of the town's zócalo,
where abuelas came to pray
and tourists came to photograph

flowers that smelled like after-sex
in spring, the same place my brother
tripped while running and split

skin against rock, his knee a mangle
of flesh and fat, deeper than anything
I'd ever seen, a reminder to never

disobey when Ma tells you to stop
running, and then you grow up
and understand, but back then

we only understood crying
like thunderstorms that loomed
each night, a polyrhythm duet of tin

roofs and tropical rain like we never heard
in California—the same summer
I read Kody Scott's autobiography, a Crip

who crept with OGs inside Cadillacs
bluer than any nightfall I'd ever known, aiming shotguns
at boys who looked like him, only neighborhoods apart.

Some of Our Boyhoods

Praise the older cousins, the Felipes who intro-
duced us to untouchable things: Lauryn Hill's voodoo

and the deep mouth of Nas;   the rebel
thumb-flicks of a chrome Zippo; scenes in *Full Metal Jacket*

when the soldier explodes his own
face off, before prostitutes

zombie in the darkness   promising *we love you long time.*
Where we got our cool from, pretended like we knew

what good weed smelled like,   how to slide   a condom on.
Back then, everything   was a series of pretending until we weren't

pretending anymore.   By 8th grade we stopped
doing homework and raising our hands,   instead cutting

class and cracking jokes about the Holocaust
in the back row of history.   No one

to tell us *do your work* or *don't say that*
at home.   We'd just punch and wrestle and shoot

bb guns until birds dropped from the air, heavy   with blood.
The time Jumbo's dog chewed up a kid's hamster and after

the boy cried, Jumbo told him to stop being   *a fuckin' fag.*
We couldn't watch the hamster's slow unfolding

so found the biggest rock   in the yard.

Speech Cantos

I am the tongue

transmuted—the chatter of cousins
          I haven't seen since elementary

when the world was still our widest

          kaleidoscope. In Xalapa

we ran games under corrugated roofs,

          ran fingers through silver-fished rivers,

                    ran mouths until they filled with pambazos

from tía Gracia's kitchen, a bigger-than-other-houses

house of Chazaros, with dirt
driveways and white walls to keep us in.

The same place Spanish outgrew me at ages 2, 6, 16, 22, 33

the clumsy growth
of my limbs, the spillage
of syllables.

Remind me: how does one's music
become another's wreckage?

          Say what you can't: there will always be a Felipe

to mock my accent—

          more American than having Jason Kidds on my feet.

More American than our toothpaste

suburb. More American than my sangre. Out of twelve

my dad was the first who flighted North.

A Poem While Wearing Jason Kidds

I think about not scuffing them. About my retro

Warriors jerseys. I think of *Space Jam* & Bugs Bunny crossovers. I think

taller than I really am, being half-an-inch closer

to infinity, the inner

soles cushioning my feet & ego. I think alley-oops

& boomshakalakas, pinstriped b-ball shorts & rookie

cards. I think about the slow art of getting

what you want but don't have, about Pokémon

trades inside middle school gyms. I think toothbrush-clean

sneakers, tucking jeans into creases & kneeling to wipe the dust

particles into air. I think community college & boxes

stashed beneath my bed, graff sessions

while Phife Dawg freaks a midnight verse. I think of voices

I don't hear, those who walked before me, underneath

me. I think of random spots: the Buddhist temple on a hillside,

the taco truck on 29th. I think of factories where the stitching & gluing & longest

hours stretch, how the cost of a U.S. dollar can be weighed

in the rubber on my feet & I think what it must feel like to never feel

robbed.

A Millennial Walks into a Bar and Says:

Let's start off with a Disney movie because why
shouldn't we? The one where the boy gets sucked
into the game his father created. Virtual

reality. And let's consider how there is an invisibility
to everything. How voices can break the air-
waves across oceans slapping coastlines. And let's disregard

tsunami ripples. Who takes responsibility for this, anyway?
It's an American thing to scream out *take no prisoners* in public. If not,
it should be. Think of national security threats. Unidentified hackers

who break codes. I asked my students what they think
about this and they told me about plaid shirts, the lag
of internet, *Wreck-It Ralph*. Excuse me, I've mentioned

another Disney movie I haven't seen. Honestly,
I worry about oil pipelines in North Dakota.
About congress evil-scheming behind

our noses. They are planting lemon trees
in our backyard like it's okay but this is approval
by majority so sit back and watch that shit grow. I apologize

if nothing bothers you; I am easily bothered. This brings me back
to lemon trees and oil pipelines. Doesn't it seem
like *Planet of the Apes*? What if Charlton Heston was telling us

something important when he said *I'm sending my last signal
to Earth before we reach our destination*?
That's a rough paraphrase. What isn't rough?

When they discovered neon it was accidental.
When they discovered continents it was accidental.
When they discovered us it was accidental.

Maybe not. Maybe I'm saying history
isn't orchestrated by a perfect god.
We are byproducts of earthquakes. And English

is commonly spoken everywhere. Does anyone care
it started with rape? Often,
I speak in another voice. Maybe

it's yours. I apologize. I apologize
for apologizing so much. In the 1940s
a group of teenage boys were tested

as experiments by the SS. I learned about them
while touring a death camp in Oranienburg.
How the Germans kept them for *scientific purposes*.

How those boys outlived the German lieutenants. Poetic
justice, some might say. Meanwhile in the South Bronx, teenagers
built cultures from wax while DJing inside broke

down project buildings and spitting fluids into crowds
who kept their hands up until the break of dawn. A breaking
dance motion. Contortions of the spirit. Head spins. Nothing

like U.S. military drones missing their targets. Nothing.
But everything like jazz quartets. In New Orleans
there are streets that have retained the noises of ghosts:

Tchoupitoulas; Calliope; St. Claude. Find me
there. I want to remix the wrongs and make a mixtape
of imperfection. I want to put this in your stereo

and let your older brother get drunk to it, let your grandmother
fall asleep to it. Dreams are the origin of an end. Think
about the flying cars and robots in movies, how they act and move

fakingly real. Am I wrong? I really can't say
I'm Mexican just as I really can't say
I'm American. Someone built this bridge between me. They carved

hyphens from the air for me to cross. Not just the crossing
you might be thinking of. But the sort that can birth multiples:
national borders, puzzles, holy crucifixions, movements

across disparate bodies. I apologize again. I just did that thing
when you use a word in your definition to define another word. But I'm sure
language is empired from mistakes so I'd rather

not take this to you. It might stifle what my friend Stan
calls *moon-guzzling*. Instead, keep jogging until you reach the edge
of yourself. Jump off. And find pleasure between your falling

breaths. The week before Obama's presidency ended we drove
to Half Moon Bay. 80s synthpop and a flood
of lo-fi on the stereo. I found a decayed bunker on a cliffside

with aqua graffiti letters that spelled *INNA TRIBE*. Yesterday,
I ate ribs at a mom and pop's in South Hayward. The talk of teaching,
of weddings, the slow goodness of slow-cooked BBQ inside us. Nobody

flinches. Imagine Tongo and MK Chavez hurling poems
at the heads of protestors in our streets while something burns
in the near distance; strange horizons to remind us of unbroken nights;

a reminder to drive slow and pump your brakes; old school Kanye;
Shakir from the Lower Bottoms singing Italian operas at California
house parties. Not like what you see on television. Or maybe

it is. We were born here and raised up like the Redwoods. Who asked?
Moving on, our neighbors are new and the old ones just moved out.
Not always by choice. How do spaces change over time? It's just time

they say. I don't talk with Ma much because she bounces around,
this time to LA. Video games are her pleasure. In *Dragon Age Inquisition*
she plays as a character who hunts dragons and has sex with other players—

she explained this to me, though I've never owned a PS4. In *Wired Magazine*
you can read about two sisters from Seattle, ages 9 and 11, who built a Do-It-Yourself
spacecraft from simple materials and used a GoPro to capture its ascent

into the blindness of space. It's all on YouTube. I wonder
if our imaginations become wrinkled and weary with age. I wonder
if things are really things. I bet all things eventually change

when resisted (i.e. Civil Rights). How this can all pour
from my fingers in a matter of minutes like outdated
newspapers. We mostly use Twitter as a source of news anyways.

Entertainment doesn't hide itself from us very well. At the gym,
why do we look so discomfortable? At bars, why
do we look so discomfortable? This is rude of me to ask on a first date,

I've been told. Perhaps the salad would have been a better choice.
Locally foraged, says the 8-pt. font menu. Some of us would rather eat strawberries
at home while watching Trevor Noah. Note to self: do this on a Wednesday night.

Self-Portrait as American

I say *fuck*
because it feels right
about now,
and I say *love* because
what wrong
could it bring?
I haven't shot a pistol
since my stepdad
flung his Desert Eagle
from the bedroom and took us
to burst freedom as kids.
The smell of sulfur
and devil, the pinch
of steel between my 10-
year-old fingers. I didn't
seek this, was never good
at hitting body-
sized targets,
kept my eyes
shut while I curled
the trigger. It's heavier
than you think,
to hold and re-
lease thunder.
Not like the movies but
somehow like the movies.
Ears still ringing,
vibration
in my bones.

Broken Sestina as Soundscape

How the room never danced because Pa never played
Juan Gabriel or other Mexican vocalists
in our house. After crossing the border,
he must've ditched a suitcase of himself at U.S. Customs.
Or maybe he never carried that suitcase. Maybe he wasn't mixed
about raising boys in a middle-class neighborhood,

assimilating to cul-de-sac neighbors
so we could run outside with footballs and play
like all-Americans. In elementary school, I mixed up
my place, sat next to Danny and Michael until my voice
forgot its own music. I became accustomed
to whiteness, neglected the border's

motherhood. I used to doodle in English, on the borders
of my notebook, before I visited Pa's childhood
home in Xalapa, before I knew how uphold the custom
of folding tortillas with every bite. I never heard Pa play
Spanish music, never caught him wandering the vocals
of a Vincente Fernandez song. He never mixed

his past with our pleasure, preferred the mixture
of elegance and fine dining in American downtowns. He bordered
on being white-washed, dreamed he'd be seen by the locals
who owned town homes around us. He loved our neighborhood,
never wanted me to leave, was probably scared I'd play
around and discover earthquakes. I did. Customized

myself by learning how to change into costumes
when needed by blasting hip-hop. I have mixed
feelings about not recognizing Pedro Infante's lyrics, about playing
more Tupac than mariachis. I've become a borderland
of tongues, a mezcla of eyes. I navigate unknown neighborhoods
and follow the rhythm of inner voices

telling me to move past myself. Most days I feel voiceless
and misguided in my body, accustomed
to breakages. But I've learned how to break different neighborhoods
open and let oceans swim inside me, a mixtape
of blood and knuckles swelling against these unbordered
soundscapes, something new in my stereo always playing.

Ode to Kendrick Lamar

There are nights like tonight when it rains / biblical amounts of everything and music

plays while I drive somewhere I usually don't / go after dark because I get lost

in my head / while my wife plans for next week and I try to decide where

to park and when to / leave but instead I down / IPAs and smash In N Out burgers

into my gut before the smallest / words crawl out / forced. Some days I feel the dark

rushing / a tidal wave of fuck / you's cresting my insides. / I double-knot my Tims

and avert eye contact in a hoodie and baseball cap. / I am not this

façade / have never sailed a fist into a stranger's / skull but there is a thunderstorm /

coming and I must know my way. Tomorrow / I will drive a pickup to the end / of the

road on the other side of 880. I will park and read / poetry while 18-wheelers rumble

within inches of my chest. It is what excites / and repels my attention while riding this /

neighborhood. How the blood of sweet grass reminds me of something else.

These Hours Are So Colored and Wasteful

We all carry certain amounts of piñata

inside us, stringed to whatever tiny or giant

truths we've tied ourselves to. Nowadays, there is so much

dangling that I've forgotten the vowels

crutched inside my mouth. Question: what would you say

if I were California's Redwoods and you were the morning

frost clinging my branches? Explain the machinery

of whalebones and the circuitry

billowing our ribs. I want to believe that

there is still electricity in my blood. That there is more

to our days than these colored and wasteful hours

being vultured. Give me what's next—

the uncrossed canyon in your hands.

Summon the perfect hit. I need to know:

would you rather crawl in your own thirst

or feast through my starvation? *Swing*,

they said.

How to Watch Mexico vs. U.S.A Soccer with a Father Who Is More Referee than Coach

1st Half:

Ask easy questions   you already know
he'll answer: i.e. *Was that off-sides?*
Is that   a penalty shot?   Can
you get ejected for dirty   slide tackles?

Understand that   this game is played
inside a rectangle,   that a rectangle
is   unchanging ,   that   boundaries
are   in place for   a reason.

2nd Half:

All I know about Pa's first
wife is a photo
I found. Her
blonde curls, blue eyes, waist-
line sharper than I'd imagined.
She was more than I believed
he could hold, her American
arms silking around his skinny
shoulders like I've never seen
before. She stands above
the orchids and mud-heat, wearing
independence like an heirloom
necklace. I've never known her, cannot
make up her scents, am foreign
to her pink-flesh lips, tasting
of different salts. I only know
her name was Connie, that she was
an open road splitting
North. Over decades,

she's become the silence
of the passport inside my luggage,
her citizenship calling
me into unknown fields.

Lesson on Manhood

We'd go to East Side San Jose to visit Pa's friend

with the sky-blue Mustang in a garage with ripped

pages of women in bikinis taped

to the walls. He told us about 289s, 302s,

351s, how he'd excavate them from inside

rusty Fords like salvaged treasures. We learned

how numbers meant the cubic-inch size of an engine—

your manhood throttled beneath the hood.

We traced the curves of '68 Cougars, '69 Galaxies,

dipping into the oil-greased argot of gearheads with

questions of what made an inline-six an inline-six.

Teenagers, we'd later race down El Camino

in our parent's cars, bragging when we didn't

crash. While carburetors cooled we'd jaw

about saving up for the biggest muscle on the block,

knowing it was more than we could wrangle. Eventually,

the mechanic married and had a kid. Eventually, he became

oil dripping through a filter overnight.

Eventually, he only flashed his ride from underneath

a tarp instead of the shoots on 101. One day,

we stopped coming back.

Julio César Chávez vs. Oscar De La Hoya, 1996

That night our apartment was an armpit, testosterone
and sweat-washed as if Papi and his friends were the ones

entering the ring. When he let me sip his Heineken I knew
it was a big deal. I stumbled and hiccupped, imitating Dumbo

from the Disney movie I loved. The men laughed, easily
entertained until Chávez appeared on screen. The *Mexican*

Warrior, they called him. Papi reminded me
how he had battled one hundred fighters, more

than Ali, or Tyson, or Dempsey. Then De La Hoya
entered. Everyone booed, telling him to go back

to his locker like the traitor he was. The Mexicans
thought he was gringo and the gringos thought

he was Mexican. I should've smiled
with missing front teeth for *the Golden Boy*

in his mixed-up outfit, a combo
of U.S. and Mexican flags, but I didn't. I don't

remember the actual fight, a flurry
of blurred punches and card girls in bikinis. I wasn't sure

what took place until everyone started
grumbling, their movements a beer-confused

disappointment. I swear a man even cried. Chavez
was hunched over in his corner, right eye swollen

from repeated jabs to the brow, while De La Hoya
stood center, undefeated.

Californiacantofunk

all-black Chuck Taylors

      because red or blue
meant you could get jumped like Gesem

on California Street even if you looked

      like me: shaggy hair, baggy shorts, skater
wannabe, back when we'd let loose
      and cruise

      with 40s near freeways
on weekdays because we never did

               homework

         how could we

      stay cleaned up
growing up in the Bay?
      drive around and see
      graffiti on fences

housing complexes where familias
rented bounce houses for birthdays
every weekend blasting music from parking lots
         everyone's invited

      our first apartment full of immigrants—
Vietnamese, Korean, Filipino
      none like my family, all of them
         like family

behind the school with Samoans and Blacks, Persians
and Russians, bodies
broken and poured into these neighborhoods

where we never knew
ice never saw snowfall
        unless we tripped
out to Yosemite or Tahoe
        whenever primos visited
from beyond Nevada or Texas
but never snowboarded because
it was too expensive

                back home
                    with cockroaches
            and bumble bees in empty fields
                    don't get stung
            by Super Soakers

in places where E-40 and Andre Nickatina
        made us slump in backseats

twisting our Ws and blunts
coughing lungs until the sun came up

        the time we climbed to the top
of an abandoned building by 101 to overlook
the jigsaw beneath us
our kingdom
                we wanted more

        Pacific Ocean at night
Santa Cruz and Sublime, barbeques
on beaches, hope we don't crash

the summer dizzies

        our skin always killing
        the December air

                    on Christmas
eating tamales and playing catch
with cousins, another barbeque

wouldn't you?
        why wouldn't we
stay out of pocket, burn rubber

at intersections, home of the hippies
and hustlers, where you'll see a dude
eating a French baguette
        and smoking a Black & Mild
        at the same damn time

one   in each hand,
jeans below his waist,   middle
of the day, metaphorical
finger up

                        in Safeway parking lots
beneath isolated stars, *'93 Til Infinity*
escaping the car's speakers

                        one way to experiment with virginity,
                        all of this

                in one night or every

                night

        happening or happened it's all

the same around here—

Backyard Boxing

After school we'd slip
        into the back and swing

our skinny: weak
        haymakers we thought

would make us grown
        men. I wondered

if we'd ever get sleepy
        from knocking ourselves

around empty fields,
        if we needed gloves

to shield or break
        us from each other. One

afternoon I refused
        to fight, Emilio's punches

popping my ribs and jaw.
        My arms fell mute

until the crowd lost
        interest. *Hit him back!*

they told me, as if my body
        had forgotten how to hurt.

Bricks

Near the park where we hoop
on weekends, we park the car
and spark blunts into rotation like
just-born stars orbiting black
and brown fingertips in a ritual
of smoke-dream and ash. We mix
drinks and debate about
Steph Curry, women, Wolverine, never
reaching conclusions. Bored,
we freestyle—I'm in the backseat
of Delande's Buick when a trap
song comes on and my boys
are hype. They rap *fuck bitches*
get money as I peel
my layers off, summoning
spells over trill, spitting rhombus
over rectangle. The cypher
is a loop of infinity and head nods
I never break so bless
the rhythm with intellect
on cue. Halfway through my verse
Kevin turns around and says
Nah, you need to drop
more n-ggas in that. His durag
and gold chain shine in the moon-
light like beautiful armor.
I do not tell him the word is
a brick rubbing my tonsils. That I am
more caterpillar than panther.
I do not say how the syllables carry
more oceans than my mouth can hold.
That I have tried it and drowned.
That I am too afraid to crush the darkness
and the light between us.

Pretty

We'd say *I love you, but not*
in a gay way. High school
kids, we'd only touch

through fist
& gorilla chest
affirmation of man-

hood, avoiding flamboyant
boys like we'd avoid staring
directly at the sun. Now,

grown, I look deeper
as two men inside
Davies Symphony Hall

burn into each other.
How their touch
becomes a soundtrack for their truth.

How they run fingers
in each other's
hair & rub rough neck-

lines like no one else
is alive. Are they unafraid
when saying *I love you*?

It seems orchestral,
boundless, how they merge—
head on shoulder,

hands in laps, lips
slightly apart. *Pretty,*
someone might call it. I say

someone because to say *pretty*
would be *hella gay* of me
& since middle school

I've been taught to never use
umbrellas when it rains, to never
pull from inside

yourself for explanation, to never turn
at angles that might expose.
So how do you expect me to say *pretty*?

Litany, Ending with Night

The morning air is spiked

with thorns—I am not able to walk

through fire though maybe I have

tried—shame is a parade

of licking tongues and everyone is

invited—ask me if I am

redefining what I know or retracing

false contours—ask me if shadows

are empty or reveal

what is already there—

the translation of being naked

is certainty mixed with

uncertainty—have you ever prayed

in your abuela's tongue? —

there is a sun and a moon

dogging every battlefield—

there is a broken window

inside all of us—the vibes are similar

to "White Ferrari" blaring

from a Chevy—play this on repeat for everyone

to move with—cross the desert

drying on the shores of my lips—crash

your mouth and hipbone

against my dark—our lightning is

a superbloom of waste

flaring into night.

Piñata Theory

Blindfolded I was
given a broomstick and told to hit
a moving target.

When I swung my dizzy arms
an adult on a chair would pull
on a rope to yank the rainbow

fluff of goods beyond my reach. Everyone
laughed and sang about hitting the cardboard
carcass, but I only became more

lost. To prove them
wrong, I focused harder in the dark-
ness. ██████████████ .

X   X   X

Consider the violence
of living. How breath can be
fractured and displaced
while walking. Take bones,
for example, how they are firm enough
for everyday activity
but collapse on impact. I fear
these injuries, knowing
what's beneath, revelations.
Each day is a split in the skull,
a bang in the lungs.

X   X   X

If I am piñata then hang
me with strings of coriander
and rainbowdust while playing
retro surf music and popping
party balloons until I am

spilling myself and you are
reaching to gather whatever
part of me is unbroken.

X   X   X

Tonight is a cliffside—

everyone is loose and dismembering
something might bring us together—

we went from smashing Spidermans
to smashing institutions we can't see—getting our spins

and tumbles from tequila and Sierras,

pretending to be ourselves but never
trusting the brakes—a different kind

of broken—a slower waking
up—each morning becoming

more monster—needing a harder
sort of destruction—

X   X   X

        This glue was never meant to hold us

together. / We were covered in layers

        of pretty colors, papier-mâché faces, / superhero

assemblages of warehouse scraps. / Beneath

        Robocop exteriors, we stomach

lollipops, / our breakage a celebration. / The truth?

        We were made for beatdowns.

Break

Break

Break

Break

Break

Break

Break

Break

Break

Break

Break

Break

Break

Break

Break

Break

Break

Break

Break

Break

Break

Break

Break

Throw Away the Cowboy Shirts

Like other men, he secreted himself
North so he could own a Chevy
and drive over paved roads.

To his wife and five kids
back in Durango, he flickered
until fading. Nothing

but his side of the mattress
and some extra plates to remind them
a father once lived there.

In the East Bay
he worked under the table, a cash-
only laborer. Eventually

he married Briana's grandma, an American—
native—her skin dark and leathery
as a bargained purse.

He couldn't speak
English, didn't know what his name
meant: Fortunato.

A borracho.
Could build a wall a week
after he tore the old ones down.

And a gambler, too, out late
with the guys in the back shed,
smoking and singing and pissing

on grass he mowed that after-
noon. Mornings, he stumbled
home with sex and tequila

on his mustache, barking
why breakfast wasn't ready.
He was lucky: Fortunato.

Bragged about the time he punched
a cop, only to be bailed
out of jail by a woman.

Once—when he upset grandma
like often, like oceans—
we threatened

to call Immigration.
But how could we—
the children of immigrants

ourselves?
We didn't want him living
in our house,

at our parties, using
our toilets, our hand soap.
One night when he left

to get drunk, a cousin
crouched over a pile
of clothes inside his room

and pissed, his unofficial
send off. For months her urine
clung to the collar of his cowboy shirts.

Glitch

The night entered me at a bar

in Oakland and I learned that

East Bay is pig Latin for *beast*

and sometimes the hills are coyotes

burning in their sleep and tonight

we need this moon between us

but who knows where this smoke

will lead and try listening to the deep

whistle of a sequoia and know

these Nikes make me feel royal

and curse minimum wage because

forever is tomorrow and today

will fade you without clippers

and patterns will form wherever

you let them because what is

a formula if not this and

who will breathe if you cannot

and where do things go after they are

buried and if the bible was really truth

why does our blood hymn and I ask

about the body and I ask as if

you know what I am praising—

Google Searching Mexico

I — "consider very carefully whether you should go"

What you might expect:
beers on a beach, tan lines
and margaritas. The coast
of Puerto Vallarta is choked
with tourists. I am
approached by a street
vendor selling only
phone chargers and selfie sticks.

II — "government advises against non-essential travel to Mexico"

My brother was robbed once
in Guadalajara, a gun's jaw
pointed at his. Summers after,
I visited. For some reason
my Levi's and Nikes
didn't loose the devil.
I ordered tacos, chewed slowly.

III — "Areas affected by the Zika Virus include Mexico"

Do you know what it feels like
to be the always-American cousin?
The one who grows
violins inside his stomach
after eating nopales in Zacatecas?
Whose ankles become piñatas
for mosquitos in El Castillo?

IV — "Level 2, Practice Enhanced Precautions"

I don't live with dust in my eyes.
I have a hobby of getting lost
in Guanajuato, of climbing

stairs made of mountain
stones and daggering into alleyways
draped in dark.
I walk with my eyelids
closed, ask strangers for
directions, keep my phone
on airplane mode.

V — *"latest figures show the number of murdered U.S. citizens south of border has gone up"*

In Aguascalientes I carried the moon
under my arm and the stars
in my back pocket. I dreamt
of turquoise and tasted silver,
snorted chocolate and prayed
inside over-visited
churches. I became the clouds
cottoning skies before rainfall,
a man riding his bike
made of bronze.
I live with electricity in my lungs,
with wings made of wood to lift me.
I build bridges with eyes of mosaic
and fumble tongues inside my mouth.
Do not tell me this is not home.

An Inventory of Cultural Fragments

Tío Gerardo in a Dodge Caravan playing
Chavela Vargas. Caballos without
saddles flowing fields. Frijoles
con tortillas y queso for breakfast.
Bus rides from Guadalajara to Teo-
caltiche. Guitaras fluttering
near the quesadilla ladies.
Faded announcement on walls. Murals
made of iron and fuego. Soccer
jerseys soaking summer sweat. Poetry
in Spanish with broken English
translations. Broken windows.
Cathedrals gold-plated. Agua
de jamaica y tacos de arrachera.
Mezcal inside jazz clubs.
Crickets inside my mouth. Salsa
brava. Policemen with pump-
actions. Fountain plazas at midnight.
Abuelo asleep in the front room.
Dormant volcanoes. Flowers
that wouldn't survive the north.

Lucha Libre, in Two and ½ Parts

La lucha:

Wouldn't have been as bad as you / I / they

think. Mexican me could've known the highest

      ceilings of tío Enrique's house, could've studied

the careful architecture of UNAM's libraries like tía

Carolina. Mexican

          me might've been more

          listo than American
          me,

might've loved mas facil than American

             me. Mexican
             me

might've understood *blood*

      as another word for *tenderness* and *tender*

as a synonym for *a pain too raw to touch.*

      I've seen Queretaro

in purple light, the city's aqueduct

      folding neighborhoods in half.

      Last summer, tía Pilar invited me to live

with her and taste the fruit

of family photo albums, each relative's

      memory my hunger.

X   *X*   *X*

El libre:

Sing the deepest song you know. The one that occupies

            the field between the countries of your body.

What I want to say is I have cousins

in Mexico, a brother in Mexico, my blood in Mexico.

      I call them *primo*, *Adrian*, *abuelo*. It's

      a privilege. To be clear, I see myself

      as privileged. In high school

        I watched U.S.A.

        vs. Mexico

on TV from my couch. I would back-and-forth

every play. I would cheer for nothing, and I would cheer for anything.

X   *X*   *X*

La máscara:

I was born in Redwood City, but my mom tells me I was born
in México. When I'm older, she shows me

a forged birth certificate with my Mexican
identity: *Alan Perez Chazaro*. In case of emergency,
she says. I've held it. The unofficially official document.
The weightless feel of something that shouldn't exist. I hold it like nothing
I've ever known.

Veracruz

Stuffed like luggage in Abuelo's '91 Bronco we groove
        over unpaved roads

toward a casita made of hay and centuries-old

earth, where gardens ripen and brown cows graze
on fenceless pastures.

On a thick-knotted mountain we pull
            up next to a house
            under construction, kicking dust
and the hot smell of livestock.

A group of chickens scatter
        as Abuelo steps into the heat, armed only
            with faded camouflage from his military
                years. My family follows, our California skin
                    no match against the Naolinco sun.

Sasha smiles, asks Ma who the home belongs to.

Aldo declares himself future owner as he puffs on a cigar, pretending
to be like our Abuelo.

Es para tu tía, el de nosotros está en Oaxaca.

        I wander off to where a rusted wheelbarrow rests
            in the shade beside well-tended nopales and tools
              with worn wooden handles covered in mud.

Abuelo finds me, lassos me
to his side,

¿Te gusta mijo?

For the first time
we embrace, a man
I've hardly know, whose brown
eyes are stronger than the knuckles
I'd been warned about, his heart
thicker than the 98-degree summer.

Si, Abuelo, me encanta.

Clinica Xalapa / Visiting Hours

I am sitting by

your side, Abuela, your breath

in this room a dwindle

of fugitive

air, a crush of the falling

clouds. Outside,

a geometry of smog and

chaos erases the stars

while I sit with nothing

clenched beneath my tongue. There is no

translation for this, no wrapping you

inside tomorrows. Abuelo waits

in the broken lobby

as I tune into the deep

hum of your bones.

X   X   X

These mountains cannot be shoveled because Abuelita

      is a forest and after

falling

we cried, and she spanked us
for crying

but she always prayed for us

(*en el nombre de el padre, el hijo, y el espiritu santo*)

because you'd better holy-cross yourself
with two fingers

(forehead, chest, left shoulder, right shoulder)

when passing a church, any church,

especially my Abuelo,
that never-faithful-macho

who always told us
eres Cuervo; translation:
you are crow

and I learned
our name is a mountain

because on a nearby mountain Abuelo
built a home for us, praying
Abuela would live to see it
from inside—

X   X   X

The breath of this land
is an orchid night passing

over a rumble of stone
roads. It's a gentle

touch, the moonfallen
undulation of hills

and banana trees swaying
in mist. It's the slow-rotting

bridge, a music wandering
around rooms where Abuelo

has hammered every inch,
has hammered bottles

of mezcal. Where nothing
shatters when things are broken

and no one notices when Adidas
have four stripes. Here, freedom rides

in the front seat of a dying Ford.

Elegy for Don Lalo's Gold Tooth

The sidewalks near Abuela's crumbled
with each step so we learned to run

the whole block to Don Lalo's bodega
where we'd snatch tamarindo and Rancheritos

from plastic shelves then pay up real quick
with small-handed pesos. He'd smile

in return, his gold tooth a flash
of every hissing summer we'd spent chasing frogs

around the hazy lagoon. We didn't know
the deepness of those waters, only that the surface

ruptured easy with the flick of a rock. When we got older
we quit drinking sodas, instead drinking

out with our cousins. Still, he'd ask when we'd return, gifting us
dulce, our American hands taking whatever

little he could offer. He never made us feel
little, our foreignness a bridge he could cross

over with. The year his family broke
the news about his burial, the streets seemed to blister

with potholes. How we'd only wanted to sprint
upstairs to Abuela's rooftop to eat our childhood

sweets again, those thick chews before a gospel
of cavities hymned themselves from our mouths.

A Pocho Boy's Mixtape

A-Side

This midday reposado has me torn and
twisted and listening to mariachis
in Tlaquepaque is the death I'm asking
for. *Siempre hay picante aquí*, my tío answers
to every question I ask. It took me awhile
to stop asking and start taking. At first it jarred
against my bones. I am no chupacabra but I've learned
every man is capable of eating, even
without appetite. Maybe I'm more obsessed
with swallowing the lies that scrape the floors
of our imaginations. Example: I visited the birthplace
of Mexican Independence in Dolores Hidalgo; I ate
a plate of overpriced arrachera in the plaza; a man
in a wheelchair asked for money; his eyes
felt empty; his palms held nothing; after, I visited
the jail cell where historians declared Mexico's birth.
I don't mean to imply we are still barred
from each other. But sometimes these mountains
make it difficult to look back.

B-Side

I'm sitting in a courtyard with Acapulco

chairs—flamingo pink, lime green—avoiding April

taxes.   I don't have to file for myself in Mexico

yet.   Back in the States, I know they'll ask for more

than my mother's peace.   What's the cost

of leaving a country to return to your abuelo's

arms?   I've walked through minefields

while somersaulting with boots, balancing

a crown that isn't worth much   but weighs more than my California household.

            Income isn't always incoming for everyone here.

Circles don't become trapezoids overnight.   They require different

angles to be muscled from the promise of each morning's

arrival.   But, who cares about simple geometry

when nothing shapes up?   My barber at Doberman's

tells me about his mother as he fades

me out;   she's a professional at cleaning up after the dreams

of European visitors at a hotel in Colonia Reforma.   My fear?

Being kidnapped by space pirates and beheaded for the syllables

inside my wallet.   It's sensationalist, I know.

But what's a peso to a dollar if they take away

        my hands?

C-Side

I dig through remixed
crates of myself, wax pressed into the grooves
of forever, then I spin that for play
like the B-Side Brujas on E. 14th. All night—
like Briana's grandma when she would hit
local clubs on San Pablo to find a Mexican

man with *nice eyes*. They come here for work,
but we work them for us. It's hard
not to romanticize the struggle of certain memories—beneath disco
lights, between cheap liquor, behind mustaches
and Camaros parked in front of the house. Our roof is shingled
but falling apart. There are parts of this neighborhood
that aren't up to code. We have a shed in the back
where Bernardo used to sleep and dreamed
of sunflowers scented in lawnmower's gasoline.
Don't forget: there are more than two sides to every story, just
like there are more than two stories inside every mouth.

On Long Distance Running

Is it because *always*
running is a cliché and clichés
are a rerun of something
realer? and since
you were a boy did they feed you
questionable instead
of *quesadillas*? and
do fat ankles
mean you are living
lavish? and isn't lavish
living a sign
of citizenship? and isn't
citizenship what some aren't
permitted?
and when you text
your homie about playing
soccer on a Saturday does your phone
autocorrect and spell
deported instead of *deportes*?
and isn't choice about going
somewhere not
always home? and why
does *orible* mean *horrible*
but never *horrifying*? shouldn't it?
and when Sergio was pulled
over by the police, wasn't he carrying
the smallest earthquake
in his palms? because wasn't he
illegal in their eyes? and don't we all
carry damaged moments
inside us like scrap-
yards and scattered wrenches?
and when can we joy-
ride California's coastline?
when we think
we know our destinations do we
really?

California is turning neon

when Kristian begins to tell me about wild rhinos

wandering Los Angeles. Once, I overheard someone

at a bar say *So much of flying is just getting off the ground*

but after you're up there it's so easy. I don't know

if I agree or if I'm becoming a smaller window of myself.

I don't know what chemicals paint this midnight. I've heard

 a white house screaming at a black one to *get the fuck off*

my block. I've circled wolves inside a strip club while a dancer

told me she wanted a *gang bang in the pussy*. It's nothing

I actually believed. When Ma told me she was sober it wasn't

half-true. Our drunken selves are mumbling

towards a beautiful apocalypse. I can smell the ghosts

of tomorrow like fumes leaking rusted pipes.

What is this architecture? Chances are

we won't meet again if we've never touched

beyond these constructed walls. Hollywood is

a chupacabra we stumble after, after hours. I've seen it

vomiting sidewalks on Spring Street.

Hunger, or What I Should've Told Briana's Grandma When She Declared We Lived in "the Ghetto"

Grace me my lover's teeth
to necklace, the gold
roping of hands

against my chest; hold
the neighbor's Rottweiler
after he dumps

piles of hot shit on our lawn;
there is no tenderness that follows
a wound; no wild-

flowers mixing in
these wildblooded streets;
last month, a group of teens

crashed a stolen car in front
of where I drunkenly parked, killing
the stop sign; our embrace

became a flash of night
inside a loosened fist,
a flickering disappearance

of houselights when suddenly
police arrived; nearby,
the Richmond marina sleeps;

I dream of unknotting
a pinstriped yacht with both of us
inside, our slow

togetherness drifting
off like the dust of some
unreachable planet;

this isn't to say I wish
to leave here; it is to say our jaws
grow wider from this unhinging.

Dear Neighbor,

it's no wonder we drive spaceships and eat
inside caves around here. Yesterday, a stranger

confessed to seeing his first murder. Said
a car pulled up his block and smoked

a dude quicker than his blunt. I don't know why
he told me this, standing at the bus stop,

but now I'm telling you. I took off
my headphones to hear him. Told him I could hear

some gunshots near grandma's street, too,
but I've never seen a body

after bullets. He paused,
his lungs a giant comma

of smoke, before offering. I told him
I'd quit. He nodded, took two

deep hits, asked what I was
listening to.

Neighborhood Watch

There is a man growing towards you
on Tennyson Ave. He is riding

a bicycle too small for his age, his face worn
down like someone's father. Perhaps

he is someone's father. Perhaps his children attend the school
across the street. Perhaps he sees you and you

see him. Perhaps there is a pause between this moment
and the next, when he dismounts. He looks around

the BART parking lot, scopes a new Mercedes and jimmies
the passenger door loose. He pretends you are

not walking past him when his hands begin to octopus
inside the glove compartment, beneath the seats.

Perhaps he does not care. Perhaps he is desperate like you
might never know. Perhaps this is something regular around here.

Burning Etcetera

The rain is drift-falling and layers

cannot save me from this winter.

On concrete, teenagers

lean against nothing, Air

Jordans laced and grounded

in a shift of faces. I've asked

if there is an art to dying

this young—if food markets

remind us good times aren't

forever. Yesterday, we arrived

to a chestpunch of dark and cups of red

sangria. We walked

to the farside until we no longer knew

ourselves, until they looked at us

for our tongues.

Pyramids have dusted here

but some still watchdog

the valley, pushing back

against snow.

My days are a murder

of time and watching

the gray slick-slide of trains.

The streets are cigarette-

stained and coffee-mouthed, tired

buildings stiffed against blue skies.

They remind me of tomorrow's

dark. The people

are friendly and speak slow

when they hear my imperfect

speech I don't know Spanish

like I know Volkswagens. Like

I know days weathered

as boot bottoms. I wander

the undersides, rub roughness

against my face. Inside

is warmest. I rest my feet

on nothing. What was formerly

a horse track in Mexico City is now

a public park. Kids and fathers

pop fireworks overhead. It sounds

like warfare. In the morning

we almost got lost

looping dirt paths. I lose myself

in new places. Where you can barely see

it, an old castillo

watches over everything. How

did it end up like this? We came

from Bone Thugs and Selena, a mix

of vibrations in our bonedust.

Rigid is the wrong word

but it follows me

everywhere. I can sketch it

onto buildings, can trace it

around rain clouds. There is a fresh-

ness I haven't known

since last night and outside is a crawl

of wood-

lands growing between us.

Feel what is missing,

make contact without

spitting.

Say *thank you*.

Say *I don't know*.

Say *did you hear that noise?*

These walls are not

really walls. They are

cave mouths, reminding us:

WELCOME!!!

Fuck off media

Beach this way →

and I don't know why

I stay inside myself

so often and away

during holidays but I dream

good and earlier I blinked

across a border while listening to chatter.

I plucked a book from my bag and let it un-

fold, turning pages

from *Catalog of Unabashed Gratitude*

like a shovel breaking

sun-dried fields.

I palmed the roots,

if only for a split, and stopped

where the outside was a freeze

of glares. For as far as I could

drink there were barely-built

things and wargrounds where revolution-

aries foxholed themselves

the way we must foxhole our desires

at night. I need to know what it means

to be small and sober,

to hold heaviness and hustle it

throughout my bones.

These mountains cannot be overlooked. I cannot

juggle planets, cannot

press rewind and shove it all

back. Where does this weight

on my bone-ribs grow from?

There is no talk of politics

that does not upset me.

I rarely talk loud. I put these rocks

in my blood and pretend I am not

fluent in burning tongues.

Notes on Gentrification

Mornings are a rough handgrab
of silicon and the unboxing of cold.

X   *X*   *X*

Every self we have ever been
is still inside us. I was told this
in winter.

X   *X*   *X*

The sidewalks are scarred, the air
pushed back.

X   *X*   *X*

When you've lost the buildings you hold
onto the trains, the *TDK*s, the *DREAM*s.

X   *X*   *X*

Last night the city danced
with fire in her spine. Afterwards,
smoke.

X   *X*   *X*

We were invited inside. We didn't leave
until the moon did.

Before Being Deported

       Silence burns

between de-

       parting brothers

like Patron

       and Optimos

in December's

       darkness. The rest

of us circle

       around; men

watching

       men cry.

Gather

Gather

Gather

Gather

Gather

Gather

Gather

Gather

Gather

Gather

Gather

Gather

Gather

Gather

Gather

Gather

Gather

Gather

Gather

Gather

Gather

Gather

While Visiting Mexico I Bingewatch the First Season of *Stranger Things* on Netflix

with my younger cousins

and I consider multi-

dimensional travel as we make

jokes in English then laugh   in Spanish. Listen: the contour

of our night is never a slow

poison. Monsters

do not emerge from an unknown

parallax but my ellipses sometimes

require translation. Ximena shows me

what I've never known   about YouTube—how

to build

a following.   I bet the group of kids

in this show could've snuck inside   anywhere, their little

Indiana

hands never getting caught.

I wonder what would happen   if they crossed a

desert's body.

I wonder   if I have ever crossed a desert's body.

I let the television's glow

collect inside my mouth. Our music

is

quesadillas

and wi-fi inside   a bright home, firecrackers on cracked

                    cobblestone,
                    the sting

                                                          of a nopal. Our summer
                                                          is never ending. We press
                                                  play like we forgot what it means.

As in, we never leave   this room. As in, when I was
        their age

                        I ran   outside Abuela's and I don't
                        understand

                                                  what it means: to be
                                                  a stranger where the sewage
                                                          is broken; to be

remixed   into multiplicity; to take
                                                          my deepest breath before another

episode
        airs.

Self-Portrait as Cartographer

Have you ever retraced the borders on a world
map with your abuela's lipstick? Post-

colonialism is a word that means *re-hustled,*
but should never be re-Tweeted. This isn't

a political statement. The states have been on fire
for as long as they have been stated. What happens

when GPS can no longer locate what you are
looking for? I'm talking cartography,

the fog-swallow of clouds, a wandering
mathematics. Since we've come a long way

from the art of papyrus. Since we've come for more
than your blood can script. Return to your proper

homes. This land is full of forsaken places
I've never visited. What is a sign if it only points you

in one direction? How can you sleep with your eyes
open and an open road ahead of you?

Is it possible to be found when you've fallen
off the map? I've been in wilderness. I've been in fluorescent

cities. I mean this literally—how the lights raged
across both places. I know the silence

of hands that can draw worlds and hands
that won't even try.

Leaving Footprints on Waterfalls

There is a voice telling me to hold chocolate

inside my mouth. I don't know what it means.

Like I don't know how lines can break us

apart. I mean this literally. How borders

are thresholds of the imagination. How

some can be crossed. In dreams I wonder

what is real that isn't shared with others.

How we share memories like sweet bread.

How sweet bread crumbles when shared.

How the word *me* lives in *America* and

in *Mexico*. How I am a forest that grows

during wildfires.

Photosynthesis (Chinaka Hodge Hosts a Block Party)

Everything begins by absorbing hydrogen   from dirt as DJs
      spin 90s r&b   with weedsmoke, and wet skin

becomes the oxygen of our bodydance—and it begins
      with inhalation: roots; rhubarb;
          sunflowers; the hot

              stench of chicken mess;
                  a thick aerosol

of summer paints; fat

Adidas laces and barbershop fades; the mixing
of light with dark and dark
      with darker. I'll say the names

      of these neighborhood trees out loud:

Southern Magnolia, Maidenhair, Chinese Flame, Kentucky Coffee

      and I'll ask what our cosmology is

if not this—and when I say cosmology know
                            I mean blessings,
                    and when I say

blessing, I mean this Sunday afternoon, because darkness is a prayer that must come

over us, it is the promise of empty parking lots
filled with movements that can be traced
back to foot-stepped rhythms and chain-link fences, the neon
blaze of a nosering on a woman's brown nose—

and it begins
      by observing the astronomy of our limbs while

remembering to sip whatever slow-
honey is poured from your lips

      like the garden in my throat

as your voice
                becomes this shovel   becomes my hands

        digging your waist—

Shadow Boxing

El cuerpo no es / eterno. / Hoy amanecí con todo / y nadie.
/ ¿Por qué no hablo direct-

amente? / Mis pensamientos / si pierden como perros / en
la calle. Ayer / encontre

el dios de la cuidad y ella no me conoció. / Yo quería dar
un beso / a la tierra pero

mis labios ya estaban sucios. / Un pintor me dijo que nunca
pintaba / con sus manos. /

Autos viejos nos llevan / a mañana. / Tengo una concha
adentro / de mi boca pero no

sabe / cantar del mar. / ¿Cuándo cae la lluvia, qué parte
del cuerpo se queda / limpia?

El otro país / me enseño 2+2=5. / Pregúntame / de la
alquimia. / Pregúntame si es

posible tener dos de todo. / Las flores caminan solas y mis
manos se quedan / sin nada.

Photo for My Unborn Child

I'm riding BART from the air-
port, observing what's outside,
corrugated fences with spray-
painted messages: *This Is Sacred Land;*
Fuck Pigs; Die Techie Scum.
The homes are historic
and diverse as the people who breathe

inside them, colorful and sprawling
along a muscular shore. Your mother
grew up here, on 55th, around the corner
from her cousin's tire shop and the bar
your grandpa would take her to perform
Mariah Carey karaoke as a kid
to crowds of drunken men. The shop

is closed now, and the bar boarded up
with graffiti'd wood. But the house
remains with the ceiling your grandpa
painted as the night sky. We will take you
to see it someday, so you can study
how constellations are formed
from the darkness of our mouths.

Untitled Memory

I'm parallel
parked in a red zone

      on Broadway in front of buildings

with abandoned glass,
waiting for you. No one

bothers or even notices
      my car in the tow-away.

                            It's calm,
            trafficless, nearly perfect

in Oakland. The air is zested

      with weed and piss and other residues
        of someone else's last night.

      From my woofers Frank Ocean's *Blonde*
trebles while between my fingers I flip

      a *West Coast Avengers* comic,
      circa 1984. I don't know why

I occupy this space, a penumbra of what's never been
realer. I don't resist the nearby lake, the clarity of clouds.

                     They keep me.

One Way Street in Xalapa

We rarely wandered
beyond the gate that divorced Xalapa
from the rest of Abuelita's driveway,

where we spent sweat-
candied summers kicking pelotas
into imaginary goals, playing

tag, and crying whenever
we scraped elbows. Out front
there was a one-way street

where old women walked
selling warm tortillas from a hot basket
balanced heavenly on braided

black hair. In those days, stray dogs
roamed for scraps of meat
and our attention. In those days, kids

our ages with dirtied faces would peek
to watch us laugh and chase each other in our Mickey Mouse
t-shirts. In those days, Abuela would hover

over us, a nearby moon in the kitchen window,
washing dishes, preparing
meals, and shouting at us if we ever reached

our soft American fingers through a gap
in the iron bars
to wiggle with wonder.

Acknowledgments

To my family on both sides of the border: I love you with open arms and an open heart. Thank you for allowing me inside, for cultivating, for teaching, for lifting. You gave me another tongue that can never be taken. Para siempre.

To my wife, Briana. In our thirteen years, you've seen me in all of my piñata stages—building, broken, bursting. Thanks for always putting me back together and encouraging my swing.

To the poetry familia I've grown with and learned from over the years. I'm like that late-blooming brother surrounded by your talent. Whether I've actually held a stage with you, shared a beer, or simply had the opportunity to read your poetry and be a fan, I've been a student of your game. Respect to those holding it down heavy in Latinx and POC poetics and communities beyond the pages: Rigoberto Gonzales; Jose Hernandez Diaz; Antonio López; José Olivarez; Sara Borjas; Javier Zamora; Marcelo Hernandez Castillo; MK Chavez; Josiah Luis Alderete; Norma Liliana Valdez; Gustavo Hernandez; Barbara Jane Reyes; Malcolm Friend; Kim Sousa; Micah Ballard; Douglas Manuel; Tongo Eisen-Martin; Chinaka Hodge; Brynn Saito; DA Powell; Patricia Smith; so many more—your work has all informed my sense of self. And to my Bay Area squad squad: Rose Heredia; Amanda Machado; Hernan Ramos; Chari Parla; Gustavo Adolfo Barahona-Lopez; Preeti Vangani; Sage Curtis; Danielle Bero; Rebecca Flores. You are all writers I am proud to have been influenced and inspired by while creating and re-creating this book.

Of course, muchísimas gracias to the editors and readers who believed in my poems in times of rejection. A special thanks to the following journals for publishing my work in early stages: *Acentos Review; After Happy Hour Review; Alien Mouth; BOAAT; Boiler Journal; Borderlands; BorderSenses; Cortland Review; Cosmonauts Avenue; decomP magazine; Drunk In A Midnight Choir; East Bay Review; Faultline; fields magazine; Forage; Frontier Poetry; Gargoyle Magazine; Ghost Town; HEArt Online; Huizache; Iron Horse Review; Juked; Loss Lit; Lunch Ticket; Matter, A Journal of Political Poetry; minnesota review; Otis Nebula; Packingtown Review; Public Pool; Rise Up Review; Split Lip Magazine; Stars + Lines; Vassar Review; Winter Tangerine.*

Some poems in *Piñata Theory* were originally published in my debut chapbook with Black Lawrence Press, *This Is Not a Frank Ocean Cover Album*. Hella big thanks to BLP—such a generous, patient, and helpful team to work with on multiple projects. Your press is opening so many doors for me. *insert praying emoji hands*

"Ode to Kendrick Lamar" and "Broken Sestina as Soundscape" appear in *Break Beat Poets Vol. 4: LatiNEXT*. Big shout out to the editors of that anthology—Willie Perdomo, José Olivarez (x2), y Felicia Rose Chavez. It's a dream to be included in this ultra mixtape. For real.

And to the professors and classmates and homies who've guided me in building then breaking these poems again and again. You've helped me find and hit targets I didn't know were in front of me as a person and as a writer. Here's to those times when we could go around San Francisco smashing Trump piñatas and shouting our poetry into megaphones. Much love. I see you, always.